Water Safety

by Jane Bellfield

Table of Contents

Chapter 1
Fun in the Water

It is a hot summer day. You want to cool off. What do you do? Find some water! A swim in cool water is great on a hot day. Or maybe you would like to spend a fun day on rides at a water park.

The one thing you always need to do in and around water is to obey water safety rules. These rules keep you from having an accident.

⚓ These kids are wearing life jackets to be safe in the water.

Chapter 2
Boat Safety

Boat rides are a great way to be in the water without getting wet. Follow these rules to stay safe while boating.

Wear a life jacket when riding in a boat. 🎧

Safe Boating Tips

⭐ Never go on a boat without an adult.

⭐ Check the weather before you leave. Don't get in a boat if a storm is coming.

⭐ Always wear a life jacket.

⭐ Be careful when you get in and out of a boat. It's easy to slip and fall in the water.

⭐ Don't jump around on a boat. The boat can tip over.

⭐ Don't jump or **dive** from a boat before asking an adult. There could be a rock or other sharp object under the water.

⊙ Three Coast Guard boats speed down the Hudson River in New York City.

People who have problems with their boats at sea can get help from the U.S. Coast Guard. The Coast Guard watches over the coastline and the seas.

The Coast Guard's **motto** is the Latin words *semper paratus* (*puh-RA-tus*). That means "always ready" and that's what they are!

Members of the Coast Guard **protect** boats at sea and the people on them. They watch from their boats, from lookout points on land, and from above on planes. Every year the Coast Guard helps thousands of people.

The Coast Guard also looks out for oil spills from ships. It watches for ice that might damage ships. Members are ready to rescue people if a ship looks like it is in trouble.

The people who work in the Coast Guard train hard for the important work they do. They often have to be very brave.

⊍ The Coast Guard helps rescue people every day.

Chapter 3
Swimming Pool Safety

Pools are fun for everyone. But it is important that everyone obeys safety rules.

Most public pools have **lifeguards** who help keep swimmers safe. Listen to the lifeguards and do what they say.

Pay attention in the pool area. Look for safety signs. They may look like the safety sign below.

Pool Rules

⭐ Always swim with a buddy

⭐ No pushing

⭐ No dunking

⭐ No running near the pool

☾ A lifeguard watches swimmers. Lifeguards jump in the water if people need help.

Everyone should learn to swim. Below are some tips for staying safe at the pool.

Swimming Safety Tips

⭐ Most pools have a safety fence. Stay out if the gate is locked. If the pool is open, go in and out through the gate. Make sure to close the gate behind you.

⭐ An adult should be with you at the pool at all times.

⭐ If you get into trouble, raise an arm so the lifeguard can see you.

⭐ Stay away from the deep end if you can't swim.

🔄 Adults may have fun watching children swim.

You can learn to swim by taking swimming lessons. Here's how a first swimming lesson may work:

1. First, the teacher helps students climb down the steps and into the pool.

2. She asks the students to hop, skip, or jump through the water.

3. Then, the teacher asks them to float face down and face up on the water.

A teacher helps a student float face up in the pool. ➲

4 Next, the teacher asks the students to do the dog **paddle**. The students move their arms and feet quickly to stay above water. They blow bubbles in the water.

5 Finally, the teacher asks the students to leave the pool without any help.

Chapter 4
Beach Safety

The ocean is enormous! It's also a lot of fun to paddle in, wade in, swim in, surf in, dive in, sail on, and ski on. But you need to be careful.

Lifeguards help keep people safe on large, crowded beaches.

↓ Lifeguards watch over people in the ocean.

Stay safe by always swimming at places with a lifeguard. Also, follow the tips below.

Beach Safety Tips

⭐ Every beach has different rules. Check the bulletin board at the beach. Information about the beach will be listed there.

⭐ Make sure that an adult is watching you.

⭐ Don't swim out further than you can stand.

⭐ Raise an arm if you get into trouble.

⭐ No dunking or pushing.

⭐ Swim with a buddy. Watch out for each other.

Become a Lifesaver

All lifeguards have taken classes in lifesaving. You could become a lifesaver, too. Ask your parents or your teacher about special training classes for children. These classes are held all over the country.

Chapter 5
Home Safety

You don't need to go far to have fun with water. You can have fun with water in your backyard or even inside your home.

You can play in an **inflatable** swimming pool. You can have fun running through a lawn sprinkler. You can even have fun in a bathtub full of water!

Run through a lawn sprinkler to keep cool. ⟳

One of the most dangerous things around water is electricity. Make sure your hands are dry when you are near electricity. Don't stand in water when you touch anything electrical. If you do, you may get a shock.

Electrical Shock

If someone gets an electrical shock, follow these steps:

1. Stay calm.

2. Don't touch the person who has been shocked or anything they are touching.

3. Call for an adult's help.

4. Ask an adult to turn off the power.

5. Call 911. Answer the questions that the operator asks.

Have fun with and in water. You can get in a boat, swim in a pool or the ocean, or just run through sprinklers. What you do is up to you.

Always remember the rules of water safety. They will keep you safe while you have fun.

You can have fun in the water while wearing a life jacket. ↻

Glossary

dive *(DIGHV)* to go into water head first
   (page 3)

inflatable *(in-FLAYT-uh-bul)* can be blown to
   full size with air *(page 12)*

lifeguards *(LIGHF-gahrds)* people who help
   swimmers at a beach or pool *(page 6)*

motto *(MOT-oh)* words that explain what a
   group stands for *(page 4)*

paddle *(PAD-l)* to move through water by
   repeatedly moving arms and legs *(page 9)*

protect *(pruh-TEKT)* to keep from being hurt
   (page 4)

Index

Comprehension Check

Retell

Use a Picture Chart and the photos to help you retell the information in this book.

Picture	What I Learn from the Picture

Think and Compare

1. Turn to page 8. How does the teacher help a student when he or she is trying to float face up? *(Use Illustrations)*

2. What rules do you need to remember when you swim in a swimming pool? *(Apply)*

3. Most places where people boat or swim have rules. Why do you think these rules are on posters? *(Synthesize)*